Faith, Family and Fishing: A 21-Day Devotional Journal

By
Tony Gerdes

Faith, Family and Fishing: A 21-Day Devotional Journal

Copyright © 2006 by Tony Gerdes

All rights reserved.

No part of this book may be used or reproduced in any manner without written permission except for brief quotations used in reviews and critiques.

Scripture taken from the HOLY BIBLE, NEW INTERNATIONAL VERSION. Copyright © 1973, 1978, 1984 International Bible Society. Used by permission of Zondervan Publishing House. All rights reserved.

The "NIV" and "New International Version" trademarks are registered in the United States Patent and Trademark Office by International Bible Society. Use of either trademark requires the permission of the International Bible Society.

Printed in the United States of America

Cover design: Marianne Mazurowski
Cover photography: Tony Gerdes

ISBN 1-4116-7881-8

Foreword

Like many men in our society today, I experienced divorce at a very young age. My father decided he no longer wanted to be a part of our lives, and my mother was left to raise my brothers and me. Little did I know at the time but my father's decision would prove to have a tremendous impact on my life. I struggled in so many ways because I lacked a male role model and spiritual leader.

In the search to fill the void my father left, I ventured outdoors and found fishing. There was something about fishing and being around water that calmed my soul. It still does. One day I discovered that the peace I felt while fishing was really God. God met me where I was. In the process He has helped me learn that He is the only father I need.

God continues to use fishing to teach and guide me today. One of the greatest lessons He's taught me is the importance of being the kind of father to my children that I never had.

Now more than ever, we, as fathers, must step up. God is calling us to be the spiritual leaders in the house. Our children and families are under spiritual attack, and it's time that fathers seek God's guidance and take a stance. The secular world presents many distractions and temptations that compete with our fatherly duties. Pride, position, lust, selfishness, and possessions are just a few of the things that are robbing us of what is really important, our faith in God and our job as father.

Tony Gerdes' devotional, <u>Faith, Family and Fishing,</u> is a wonderful source of spiritual encouragement for any man seeking to be the father God has called him to be. Tony uses his personal experiences with various aspects of fishing to help us examine our relationship with God and our role as father. He challenges us to let go of our past and lay down those things that are taking us away from our families.

Whether you enjoy fishing or not, Tony's devotional is sure to inspire you to dive deeper into God's word and discover His will for your life.

May His Blessings Flow,

Trevor Ruble
HOOKED FOR LIFE Ministries

Dedication

This book is dedicated to my supportive wife, Sue, and my amazing children, Shannon, Joey, Jonathan, Jordan, Jacob and Savannah, whom God has brought into my life.

May I show my love for him by loving them.

It is also dedicated to the men for whom it is written and the God we aim to serve.

Contents

Foreword

Introduction

Day One	**Thou Shalt Not Lie** (Psalm 37:4)	**13**
Day Two	**I Meant to Do That** (Romans 7:19)	**17**
Day Three	**Just the Right One** (Romans 8:4-5)	**20**
Day Four	**It Doesn't Matter to Them** (1 Corinthians 13:11)	**24**
Day Five	**Honey, it's for the Kids** (Hebrews 13:5)	**28**
Day Six	**All Creatures Wild and Wacky** (Proverbs 22:6)	**32**
Day Seven	**Fishing and Ecclesiastes?** (Ecclesiastes 1:14)	**36**
Day Eight	**Why Men Don't Ask for Directions** (John 14:6)	**40**
Day Nine	**The Best Fish We Never Caught** (Philippians 2:3, 15)	**44**
Day Ten	**Fishing is for the Faithful** (Malachi 3:10)	**48**
Day Eleven	**Are You Still There?** (Matthew 28:20)	**52**
Day Twelve	**Tangled Lines** (Psalm 51)	**56**
Day Thirteen	**The Fish's Point of View** (Ephesians 6:12)	**60**

Day Fourteen	**Ichthyology and Other Big Words**	**65**
	(Romans 8:11-13)	
Day Fifteen	**Name That Fish**	**69**
	(Matthew 25:31-36)	
Day Sixteen	**The World's Largest Fish Fry**	**73**
	(Mark 6:30-44)	
Day Seventeen	**The Jonah in All of Us**	**77**
	(Jonah 4:1-10)	
Day Eighteen	**Perfect Storms, Imperfect People**	**81**
	(Luke 8:22-25)	
Day Nineteen	**Breakfast on the Beach**	**85**
	(John 21:3-18)	
Day Twenty	**You Da Man—Part One**	**89**
	(Numbers 14:9, Joshua 1:1, 24:15)	
Day Twenty-One	**You Da Man—Part Two**	**94**
	(Ephesians 6:1-4)	
Epilogue		**98**
Appendix		**99**

Introduction

They say it takes 21 days to form a new habit. If that's true then by the end of this 21-day devotional, you're habit will be getting a deeper perspective on God's word. Not bad.

From time to time I would find myself struggling with my personal Bible reading. I would open up to a random page and start reading without any real purpose or plan. Often times God would honor my effort by sending me to passages that hit home right away. Other occasions were not as productive, leading me to get more frustrated with my spiritual stagnation and less likely to seek his truth the following day.

Devotionals have helped to give me a specific thought to meditate on during the day. Joshua 1:8 reads "Do not let this Book of the Law depart from your mouth; meditate on it day and night, so that you may be careful to do everything written in it. Then you will be prosperous and successful." I want to be prosperous and successful and I bet you do too. God just told us the secret: flood your mind with his word.

Take each day's reading and each devotional thought and reflect on them. Consider how each applies in your own life. To help with this, I've included a section at the bottom of each reading. This "Captain's Log" section is the place for your notes and reactions. It's also your action plan. You've read it and meditated on it, now do something to make it stick.

The legendary fisherman, Captain Ahab, in Melville's <u>Moby Dick</u> was dedicated. He was passionate in his pursuit of the White Whale. The thought consumed him day and night. God is bigger than any whale. But we seem content to shut him in a box about the size of a few Sunday morning hours. Pursue God with passion and a purpose: to be a disciplined follower of Christ. Proverbs 8:17 gives it to us straight, "I love those who love me, and those who seek me find me."

It's not a question of whether you will find God. He's not lost. It's all about how you pursue him. Think Captain Ahab, not Captain Crunch.

Day One

Thou Shalt Not Lie

I've heard that all fishermen are born honest, but they soon get over it.

Well, you're going to get the truth from me. The largest fish I ever caught was a 14" bass. Okay, maybe it was closer to 13 ½", but I'm rounding up. I have six children. People will tell you that I was fine with stopping after two, but God had other plans. I haven't always been the best husband, father or high school teacher. In fact, I often have struggled to be just mediocre. But Psalm 37:4 says, "Delight yourself in the Lord and He will give you the desires of your heart." I think that's how fishing came into my life.

I was never an outdoorsy-type person. (I think my wife just said "prissy.") I could handle the worms, but didn't like fish one bit. The few times I went fishing with my father were enjoyable, mostly because of the soda I'd get at the end. I found out recently that he really didn't know what he was doing either, just trying to stay a step ahead of his son. It wasn't a problem. I wasn't going very fast.

After my parents' divorce, my vision of what a father should be became obscured. Then as I began raising my own children, I found I had no direction. I knew how to perform at work, study in school, and help create children. But I had no idea how to dad.

My wife confronted me one day. She told me that it seemed as though even when I was home I longed to be somewhere else. She was right. I had moments of happiness, but no joy.

It's funny—when you hit the bottom, you can only look up. I remember lying on the kitchen floor yearning for some way out of the mess I didn't even understand. No change. Yet, I also remember crying at the altar on Father's Day one year, asking God to bring me joy with my family, so that I could be a daddy to my children and a sacrificially-loving husband to my wife. That time it took.

Slowly things began to change. My wife and I could talk more, and I resented less. I began to look for ways to spend time with my children rather than sending them away when I got home from a tough day. Honestly, I prayed that God would change my priorities so that my real job would be fathering, and my teaching career would exist to pay the bills. I sought the will of God and realized that the desires of my heart were out of alignment. God called me first to be a patriarch, not a professional.

So when Joey, my oldest son, included fishing and hiking on a list of things he wanted to do on a Saturday, I knew that I was in for it. I started with the hiking and quickly discovered that my boys were adventurous—just as God had made them. Climbing up to a rock ledge that soared 195 feet above the ground, I was starting to feel the spark of adventure firing in me as well.

Before I knew it, we were fishing. And yes, I jumped a few times as those scrappy little fish wiggled when I tried to unhook them. But I was overcome by the joy we shared. Four hours had passed and the only complaining came when it was time to leave. Praying that night with my children, they thanked God for the fish we caught and prayed for success the next time.

True, God says he will give us the desires of our heart. Regrettably, that's about as much of that verse as most people know. That fragment is so misleading when read in isolation from its true message. God has wonderful things for us—perfect gifts—so he is not impressed by our material desires. Like with me, God sometimes has to reshape our hearts so that our desires are as pure as the joy he wants us to have. He is pleased to give us what we want when we want the right things.

Now, I love fishing. I am in awe of God's creation. And I love my family. For some time I couldn't say that with any great conviction.

But God has shown me what an enormous blessing it is to have a faithful wife and loving children.

And that's the truth.

Captain's Log: We can all fool somebody, but we can't fool God. Think about yourself honestly and write down your responses. How's your spiritual life? Prayer life? Bible reading habits?

Think about your marriage and your relationship with your children. Any sore issues lingering here?

Consider your job. Do you work as if it is done for the glory of God?

God doesn't demand perfection, but he knows our hearts. He honors our attempts to improve by molding our character and our situations. So here's your assignment: take one thing you want to improve in each of these three categories (spiritual growth, family and work) and do it today. Maybe you'll be reading a longer Bible passage than normal, washing the dishes without being asked, or spending time revising that report so it's just right. Honest growth. It starts today.

Captain's Log:

Day Two

I Meant to Do That

Immediately after returning from Wal-Mart, where we had purchased our fishing gear, my children were begging to go outside and learn to cast. Although it had been more than twenty years since I had fished, I had it in my mind that I could still do it like I used to. Better, actually, since I wasn't that good when I was a kid.

I explained the theory of casting to my young anglers, as I tried to remember myself when to hold the button on the spincast rod and when to release it. Within minutes, my children were consistently casting far greater distances than I was. (But you'll read more about them later. This one's about me.) Frustration began to grow as I knew what it was I wanted to do, but seemed completely unable to do it.

Has this ever happened to you—either in fishing, or in fixing something around the house, or starting a new exercise program? Maybe you've felt this way when it comes to living out the Christian faith. The apostle Paul certainly had these feelings as he admits in Romans 7:19, "For what I do is not the good I want to do; no, the evil I do not want to do—this I keep on doing."

I don't know about you, but I like reading passages in the Bible like this. When this superstar man of faith confesses to doing the wrong thing, I feel like it gives hope to the rest of us. And honestly, I believe that's why a verse like this one appears. God created us to have free will, knowing that sometimes we'd make the right choices, and that sometimes we wouldn't. As we grow as Christians, the Holy Spirit will help guide us through these decisions so that we not only *know* the right choice but we *make* the right choice more often.

This reprogramming usually involves breaking a vicious cycle. When we are used to procrastinating, or justifying our failures, we get caught in a rut. Some overeat, some use foul language. For me, it's losing my temper. Step one on this cycle is knowing what your problem area is, maybe something you identified in your Captain's Log from the first reading.

Step two—the typical build-up—I feel my blood pressure shoot up, knowing I am ready to explode. I justify it to myself claiming the kids have really done it this time. They deserve it. (By the way, children need discipline, for sure. But they don't ever deserve to see an out-of-control, maniac father.)

Step three—I blow up like a volcano, the typical climax in my routine. Then I hear that voice inside my head saying, "What kind of Christian are you? You can't control your anger." This voice prompts step four—the confirmation. Heaping on the guilt, this voice leaves you doubting you'll ever change. If you believe the voice, confirm it, you're stuck for sure.

Paul doesn't suggest for a minute that he is stuck, however. He admits that he's human and has the same struggles that we all do, but trusts in the Holy Spirit to help change him. You've no doubt heard somebody use the expression "under the circumstances." You've probably used it yourself. But did you ever stop to wonder why someone would want to be "under" the circumstances? God's got a much better perspective for you. If you're willing to invest the effort to climb above those circumstances, the view is spectacular.

Captain's Log: What are the things in your life that you know you shouldn't do, but you do anyway? Do you see a cycle of repeating this habit, joined by shallow justification or feelings of guilt?

If you do (and we all do) then consider opening up this problem to God. Review your entry from the first Captain's Log and pray that God will help you in these areas. Remember you do have a choice. One episode at a time, I began to choose the right thing. Soon I was setting a new pattern. You can too.

A 21-Day Devotional Journal

Captain's Log:

Day Three

Just the Right One

Walking down the fishing aisle in the sporting goods store can be overwhelming. Aside from the racks of rods precariously placed overhead like elongated dominos waiting to fall, there are the rows and rows of lures. Sure, choice is good. And when you know what fish you're after, you can find just the right piece of equipment to do the job. But as a beginner, after several minutes studying the different shapes, color combinations, and hook sizes, I was ready just to grab a net and be done with it. Speaking candidly, we've had the best luck using good old worms. That's not, however, how these pros are winning tournaments, so I keep working artificial lures into my fishing day.

It didn't take me too long to learn that you don't fish all lures in the same way. Retrieving a jig like you would a spinnerbait is not what it was designed to do. Likewise, the prettiest imitation shad crankbait when fished under a bobber is not guaranteed great results. Along Richmond's James River, I was getting tired of catching tiny fish with my spinnerbait (which was designed for small fish) and decided if I wanted to catch the big fish, I needed to use the big bait. I picked just the right one and that was the secret behind my whopping 14" bass. (Okay, 13 ½".)

From the weights and floats to the line, each piece of tackle in my box was designed for a specific purpose. Only when they are used properly will they live up to their potential. My ultralight rod is great fun catching panfish in the ponds, but I'd use something different when I accept my friend's offer to land some thirty pound catfish. In a similar way, you too were designed with a purpose in mind. You have a part to play in Christ's church, and you're just the right one to do it. "Just as each of us has one body with many members, and these members do not all have the same function," Paul writes in Romans 8:4-5, "so in Christ we who are many form one body, and each member belongs to all the others." Not only do we have a purpose, but we are also dependent on each other to produce the maximum impact for the kingdom.

The church is God's tackle box. He created just the right people and gave them just the right talents and gifts to accomplish their purpose. I'm not going to try to stretch this out (evangelists are like the hooks, etc.), but I want you to consider this. Watching an angler use his equipment masterfully is a joy. There is nothing as serene as being on that water with every cast perfectly placed, every hook set. There is probably nothing so frustrating as snags and tangles in the line, or reels that decide to break when you've got a fish on the line. At times like that we stomp around, shout our favorite creative vocabulary words, and wonder why we ever left our warm beds.

For my part, I'd rather be used for the purpose I was created than to cause God to stomp around the crystal lake of heaven. Not that he would. My point is this: we don't have enough people doing what they should in the body of Christ.

At many churches, there are too many people striving for the high profile jobs, like preaching, serving on the elected church council or singing a solo for the televised worship service. Sure, some are called to these ministries, others call themselves. On the other extreme are those who don't want to be bothered to serve at all. In the middle are the very few who are responsible for making the church run, including those who would clean the church's toilets, repair the lights and change diapers. One woman told me she wished her husband would "move up" from the nursery until she realized that that's where God had put him. I'm thankful he did—the guy's terrific with our youngest children.

If you are serving your local church in the area the Lord would have you, then thank you. The Lord will reward your faithfulness. If you're not sure what your role is, pray about it. Ask God to show you. Discuss it with your pastor. Do something. God no more designed you to sit on a pew than manufacturers made those poles to sit on a shelf.

Captain's Log: Get out that pen. It's time for some resume writing. Prepare a resume listing all the talents and abilities God has given you. Discuss it with your wife. Do you see any trends? Has God prepared you for action that you're reluctant to take?

Now think about this: What would you do for God if you knew you would not fail? Each of you then create lists of up to five goals that you and your wife feel fit your God-given strengths and interests and are just crazy enough that only God could pull it off. Even the most outrageous dreams we have are nothing to the awesome power of the God we serve. So dream big! Then ask the Lord to show you what He would have you do. If you're serious, hold on; it's going to be a wild and glorious ride.

A 21-Day Devotional Journal

Captain's Log:

Day Four

It Doesn't Matter to Them

I think I'm like most guys because I want to achieve great success in all I do. Bring on the big fish. After all, I should be able to catch more than my kids. I've got more wisdom, more experience, and more patience.

One day, trying out a new pond, Joey and his friend Alexander raced over to Jonathan and me, screaming "There are some really big fish in there! One just pulled off Alexander's lure!" Here's my chance, I thought; this was going to be a good day.

Things were quiet for a while. I began to wonder if Alexander's lure had just been snagged on one of the many branches under the water. Then I heard Jonathan's voice cut into my thoughts. "Daddy, I've got one! It's bending my rod!"

I raced over to him (then raced back for the camera and back to Jonathan again). I arrived just in time to see him land a nice 9" crappie. As Jonathan was reluctant to remove the hook, Joey assisted in preparing for the photo shoot. "Nice fish," I told him. They like it when I say that because they hear it used on the Sportsman Channel, and so we sound like professional fishermen.

We didn't catch anything else at that pond, except for half of a Nerf football. So, we left that pond and went to an old reliable spot.

Although we had never caught anything of notable size there, you can feel the nibbles start as soon as your hook hits the water. It's a great place to go, especially with kids. There Joey pulled out a 7" fish that looked like something in the minnow family. Joey was convinced that it was really a baby shark.

As I relayed these stories to my wife, I commented that I didn't have a photo-worthy catch that day. Remember, I'm the one with the wisdom, experience and patience. She then remarked, "It's kind of the luck of the draw, isn't it? I mean, it doesn't matter to the fish."

Herbert Hoover put it like this: "all men are equal before fish." God put it slightly differently. In Acts 10:34-35 we read, "Then Peter began to speak: 'I now realize how true it is that God does not show favoritism but accepts men from every nation who fear him and do what is right.'" The fish don't care who it is on the other end of that line. They don't consider race, age, gender or economic status. Neither does God.

God knows the value in each of his creations. It just took me some time to figure that out. I learned God knows that the needs my children and my wife bring to him in prayer are as important as mine. What a child prays may sound cute. Committed, heart-felt praying for an invitation to a party, a new bike or a big fish, however, carries the same weight as a prayer for salvation or healing. These things are important to children and the children are important to God.

Don't be quick to overlook the power of God in our children. For me, I know my children are more biblically aware than I was at their age, even though their prayers don't sound like our pastor's. God edified his son before Jesus' earthly ministry even started, "And a voice from heaven said, 'This is my Son, whom I love; with him I am well pleased.'" (Matthew 3:17). Would you say this about your kids?

Paul reminds us in 1 Corinthians 13:11 that "When I was a child, I talked like a child, I thought like a child, I reasoned like a child." Too often, I feel an urge to push my kids to become adults: wise, experienced, patient. But if God had only valued adults, he would not have created the process of childhood. Maturity will come. Paul continues in that same verse "When I became a man, I put childish ways behind me." This time, it took some equal opportunity fish to remind me that God sees value in us right where we are.

So enjoy them, love them. Get excited about those rod-bending panfish and savor the reverence of a 5 year-old's prayers. God does.

Captain's Log: Do a quick recap of your life. Remember and record key lessons you learned along the way. Share a moment telling your kids about some crazy thing you did when you were their age. Remind them you love them just the way they are.

In addition, tell at least three people how much you appreciate them. (Your wife should be one.) Consider others like the supermarket employees, the garbage collectors or military personnel. Your life wouldn't be the same without them. In showing this rare respect for others, you will understand better how God sees us, his creations.

Captain's Log:

Day Five

Honey, it's for the Kids

There is an old fishing adage that says:
> Give a man a fish; he eats for a day
> Teach a man to fish; he must buy a boat.

Just a few minutes from our home was a small boat on a trailer, sitting in somebody's front yard. And looking very lonely, in my opinion.

My mind raced, thinking about the fun my adventurous kids and I could have on a boat. Now we could really catch some fish. The "for sale" sign listed $800 as the asking price. I'll wait—it'll go down just like the pickup truck I had my eye on whose price dropped practically every week. Of course, we still didn't have the money for the pickup truck or the boat for that matter, but I kept teasing myself that if the price got lower, I might make a move.

Sure enough, the price fell to $600, then to $500. I reasoned that this guy's wife must have told him he needs to sell it to get money for Christmas. Nobody can do well selling a boat in November. I should probably pause here and tell you that Christmas was already going to be tight in our house. I certainly didn't have $500 in cash, and hardly had that much room on the credit card. But come on, it's a boat. And after all, it's for the kids.

So, with part of me feeling sorry for this poor sap who needed to sell his boat to buy Christmas presents for his family, and part of me wondering how low he would go, I moved into the next phase of my plan. As we passed by this boat everyday, I began slyly bringing it to my wife's attention. "Oh look," I said, "they only want $500 for that boat. The price was $800."

To my surprise, she didn't recognize the obvious bargain I just laid before her. I just got a look I like to call "The Glare." It dawned on me that she felt I was being selfish. I wanted the boat because I loved fishing. My answer was to show her how noble my intentions really were.

The next time we went down that road, I said to Joey, "Hey, that boat's still for sale."

"Can we buy it, Dad?" he responded right on cue.

"All we have to do is to convince your mother," my thoughts ran on, but I kept quiet. My loving wife reminded me that I've never closely looked at this boat, that it may have a hole in it, and that we still didn't have the money to buy it.

She was right. Honestly, I had wondered about the practicality of it as well, what with the maintenance, the hassle of hooking a trailer onto my van, and driving with a trailer, which I've never done before. But it's a boat.

My step-father, who has owned plenty of boats, was fond of the expression about the two happiest days in the boat owner's life: the day he buys it and the day he sells it. Maybe it was his voice that I kept hearing. Maybe it was the Holy Spirit. Throughout all my fantasizing about this boat, I struggled because the shore fishing we had been doing wasn't so bad.

Hebrews 13:5 states "Keep your lives free from the love of money and be content with what you have, because God has said, 'Never will I leave you; never will I forsake you.'" Putting it into perspective, God, our heavenly Father, wants us to rejoice in the things we have and know that as a father; he doesn't want us to suffer need. I firmly believe that God could have easily made some provision for me to get this boat, if that were best for me, without requiring me to max out a credit card and spend several cold nights on the couch. He could have, but he didn't. Instead, he set my heart back on the right track, pursuing him and his righteousness.

How often do we correct our children for not being grateful for the things they have? "You'd better eat that because there are kids starving in Africa." Or how about, "I'm not buying you any more toys because you don't take care of the ones you have." We have our soapbox prepared and our righteous indignation masks polished, ready for the lecture that is to come.

Yet, we're the first ones to start our prayers with, "Lord bless me," followed by a list of requests so long it would make even Santa a bit queasy.

I was proud of myself that when I told my wife about the boat being sold, I felt no remorse. She did ask if I was the one who bought it, and I told her no. I began to explain how I didn't feel bad about missing the opportunity, but I don't think she heard me over her sighs of relief.

I hope that guy bought some great Christmas presents…and a really nice one for his wife.

Captain's Log: I was blessed one day after going to a local store to buy a sandwich for lunch. I was feeling so hungry, my mouth was watering. But when I came across a man who was begging for food, I was reminded that I would eat dinner that night. This fellow may not. I gave him my lunch and we began to talk. Today, share something with someone else. Then write a description of the event including your reflections. Give freely and unexpectedly. Go ahead; you will never give more than God has given you.

A 21-Day Devotional Journal

Captain's Log:

Day Six

All Creatures Wild and Wacky

Because you can't go fishing everyday (at least that's what my wife says), the kids and I had to settle for watching fish on a television program. Talk about amazing. We saw fish stalking their prey like hunters in a tree stand. The boys loved the ferocious, ripping attacks of the sharks. My favorite, however, was *Protopterus annecten,* also known as the African lungfish.

The program explained how this specie lived in riverbeds that would often dry up due the intense heat and arid conditions. To survive, it would curl up into a cocoon made up of its own mucus. As the outer shell of the cocoon hardened, it would slump into a kind of hibernation until the rains came. In one segment, the block of dried mud that held the cocooned lungfish was used as a brick in a wall. When the rains returned, we all watched in amazement as that fish slipped out of the wet brick, down the wall and into the newly re-created river.

Fishing is a great way to teach your kids about stewardship and respect for God's creation. After watching this show, we talked about the different abilities God gave to these fish. I remarked about the care God has shown toward his creations and reminded my kids that we should do the same.

Similarly, when we go to our usual pond, I am strict about cleaning up the candy wrappers and about proper handling of the fish we release. Personally, I think that if more people acted as if God created the world and all its creatures, we would put a lot of environmentalists out of business. I know that Genesis can get a bit boring when you go through all of those "begats," but you don't have to go very far in the book to see where God made the sky, the rivers and the fish. These three things alone will provide many hours of conversation as you head out with your young anglers.

Futurists predict that we will increasingly be drawn to water-based recreational activities. Like a good steward, it is imperative for us to handle our resources carefully. Ancient societies seemed more appreciative and more respectful of the world made for them. But today, in our techno-driven culture, we'd rather pollute and chemically treat our water than practice balanced conservation. We need to teach our kids about managing our environment so that we'll have a chance to fish with our grandchildren.

Proverbs 22:6 is one of my favorite passages: "Train a child in the way he should go, and when he is old he will not turn from it." This applies to all aspects of life, from fishing to family structure, so that they can live a life that God blesses. Respecting God's creation is certainly part of that. After all, Genesis 1:1 begins "In the beginning God created."

It is our responsibility as fathers to teach our children, not leave that to the public school system or television. Usually, these influences make our job harder, since their teaching contrasts with the word of God. In order to counteract these potential negatives, our children need to see what we believe and not just hear about it on a Sunday morning. To that end, think about how you are showing care for the things of God, including the church and the earth he created. Today's Captain's Log may help get the ball rolling.

Captain's Log: Organize or participate in a clean-up day or kids' day at your local fishing spot. Teach your kids how to take care of the places we often take for granted. There are many resources online you can check out if you want help. From environmental agencies to fishing ministries, like Hooked for Life, you can find someone who has experience in such events.

On a more simple scale, spring or fall clean-ups around the church are just as effective. When one of my sons got gum on the sanctuary carpet, I had him first apologize to the woman who cleans the church, then ask her for help in removing the gum. He got the supplies from her and did the work himself. It made a huge impact. He is far more responsible (especially since the church got a new carpet!)

Use the space provided for notes to plan your event and for a brief description of what you did.

A 21-Day Devotional Journal

Captain's Log:

Day Seven

Fishing and Ecclesiastes?

It was a brilliant day in Richmond, Virginia. The weather was warm with a slight breeze. I had made my familiar journey across the footbridge to Belle Isle to the spot where I caught my "trophy" bass. As I stood on the bank of the James River, I felt a bit guilty about this new job that allowed me time to fish in the middle of the day. The guilt passed with every cast that sailed off my reel and was replaced with gratitude. I smiled.

In the distance I could hear shouts and screams. Having taught for several years in a Baltimore City high school, I had learned to blot these distractions from my mind. It wasn't near me, didn't concern me, and wasn't going to disrupt my quiet solitude on Belle Isle.

I later heard sirens. Must have been an accident, I thought. Then I saw fire trucks. Must have been a big fire somewhere, I reasoned. Maybe I'll see it on the news tonight. The pieces started to slowly come together as I saw all of these emergency vehicles stopping on the other side of the river, near the base of the footbridge I had crossed. For a moment I wondered if I was in a dangerous spot, if something was happening to the bridge and I would be stranded.

Just then, I saw small groups of people collecting on the footbridge and the vehicle bridge above, looking down into the river. I soon saw the reason for all the commotion. A woman had fallen some thirty feet from the bridge onto the rocks and shallow water below.

I saw the rescue teams prepare their inflatable boats, run safety lines and set off to save a life. I saw the woman's body being secured into a head and neck brace. I saw the boats carefully deliver the woman to a waiting ambulance, which sped off with a resounding siren I could not ignore.

I didn't feel much like fishing after that. It somehow seemed inappropriate. I made my way back across the footbridge and thought. The book of Ecclesiastes kept running through my head. "I have seen all the things that are done under the sun; all of them are meaningless; a chasing after the wind" (Ecclesiastes 1:14), Solomon writes toward the end of his life. Here was a man who had the wealth of a Bill Gates, for lack of a better comparison, who could use his custom-made, gold-plated fishing tackle on any body of water he wanted. Still, Solomon calls it, "meaningless."

I thought about what I was doing there, toying with fish I wasn't going to eat, waiting for my next meeting that day. Meaningless? Sure.

The woman was blessed. She lived. For me, there wasn't a doubt to my survival that day, just like most days I wake up. But it was a sobering thought to realize that I hadn't done anything for God that day. I hadn't read my Bible. I hadn't really prayed. I hadn't witnessed to anyone.

Now Solomon doesn't say we should all be miserable, feeling condemned for our pleasure time. Chapter 5, verse 19 reads "when God gives any man wealth and possessions and enables him to enjoy them, to accept his lot and be happy in his work—this is the gift of God." That day, I thanked him for this gift and for the breath in my body, and pledged to use my days well.

Will I give up fishing? No. But God does want us to remember there is a "season for every activity under heaven" (Ecclesiastes 3:1). (I promised my wife and The Byrds I wouldn't start singing now.)

Like many men, I can get obsessed very quickly. The blinders go on and all I see is the obsession. This can be helpful when I am determined to complete a task, but not so good around the house. Shockingly, my wife doesn't feel compelled to watch fishing programs on TV and read fishing magazines all while completing a thorough inventory of the tackle box. So, when I get that look—you know the one I mean, you get it too—I remember that there is a time for fishing and a time for cleaning the dishes.

And thank you, God, that you've given me dishes to clean. The woman from the bridge would have much rather been in a kitchen than a hospital.

Captain's Log: Thank God for your life. Right now.

I don't care what else is going on in your world right now. God has kept you alive for a reason. You may not know why, but God does. Life can seem meaningless when we climb that ladder of success and find it's leaning on the wrong wall. So, "enter his courts with praise" (Psalm 100:4). Focus on God to renew your focus on life. Thank him for being all he is: Alpha and Omega, the great I AM, Jehovah Jireh (our provider), King of kings and Lord of lords. Write a prayer of praise today. Don't ask for anything—just tell God you're thankful for who he is.

Captain's Log:

Day Eight

Why Men Don't Ask for Directions

The simple answer: men know where they're going. For centuries, man has been purpose-driven—to hunt, to farm, to pick up milk and diapers. We're big picture thinkers, so we don't have time to get bogged down with the little things like landmarks or street signs.

When I was traveling to a school for a meeting, I knew my purpose, I knew where I was going. Therefore, I didn't need directions. That is, of course, until they moved the school. Really—I drove up and down the street looking for my last turn before the school and I couldn't find it. It just wasn't there. Fearing I would be late—I admit it—I asked for directions. But the guys in the gas station seemed more confused than I was. I started in the direction they had pointed, and then decided that I still knew more than they did. I took a chance on a street with no name and found myself pulling up to the school right on time. My anxiety subsided as a slight swagger returned. See, I knew where I was going.

The bad news is that many men do the same thing when trying to get to heaven. "All roads lead to the same place," I heard one politically-correct minister say. Really? When we go to our usual pond on a county park, you'd better know where you're going. Otherwise you won't know which dirt road to take. (They're not big on directional signs.) Not all roads lead to heaven. The good news is that you don't have to gamble on some no-name street to get you there. Jesus put it plainly: "I am the truth the way and the life. No one comes to the Father except through me." (John 14:6)

You see, you can't get to heaven on your good looks, fishing ability or intelligence. You've got sin and there is no sin allowed in heaven. God is holy and just and won't tolerate the least bit of corruption in his heavenly courts. "But I've lived a good life. I'm not a murderer or anything." Ever told a little white lie? How about look at a woman with lustful thoughts charging through your mind? Ever stolen, even when you were a kid, or thought that the office wouldn't miss that pack of post-it notes? Well welcome to the club, you lying, adulterous thief. You've broken three of the Ten Commandments and your chances for slipping through those pearly gates aren't looking too good.

But it's not over yet. God has made a way for you because God made you and he loves you. You don't want your kids to get hurt and neither does God want us to suffer the judgment we deserve. He sent his son Jesus Christ to take that punishment for us. It was a brutal death. But in the end, Christ stormed through the pits of hell and rose again and cleared the way for us to do the same. So no matter how far down you've been, Jesus has been there too. Better yet, he has made a road for you to get out of that place and join him in heaven.

Maybe you've heard this all before and you're already serving the Lord. The next time you go fishing with some buddies, ask them if they know where they're going. They'll think you're talking about your usual fishing hole. If they respond yes, ask them if they know the way to heaven. Then give them the directions according to the Bible. There's no reason why fishermen can't win souls today like they did in Jesus' time.

If you've never asked Jesus to be your guide, consider doing it now. It's easier than using a spincast rod. Pray something like this:

> Jesus, I know that I've done wrong things in my life. I know that I can't make it to heaven on my own. Lord, I believe you died on the cross and took the punishment that was meant for me. I believe you rose again so that I too could have eternal life. Forgive me, Lord. Wash

me of my sin. Be my savior. I thank you for making me a new creation. In Jesus' name, Amen.

If you prayed it and meant it, God will do his part. "If we confess our sins, he is faithful and just and will forgive us our sins and purify us from all unrighteousness" (1 John 1:9). Now, you're on the road to heaven.

It's nice to know where you're going.

Captain's Log: Jump to the back of the book. Read Revelation 21:1-8. (Don't worry, the surprise won't be lost when it actually happens.) Try to get your mind to picture the scene described in this passage. A new heaven. A new earth. "He who overcomes will inherit all this, and I will be his God and he will by my son" (Rev. 21:7). Use this to spice up your answer to "Why are we going to church again, Dad?"

How do you feel reading about heaven? Does it bother you that some friends and family members may not be there with you? Record your thoughts.

A 21-Day Devotional Journal

Captain's Log:

Day Nine

The Best Fish We Never Caught

There are some times, although not often enough, when a father feels he must be doing something right. It could be a sudden, unsolicited hug, or a peek at a sleeping child. Times you feel like it's going to be okay. Times you feel you should put the crowbar of correction back in the closet...until next time.

I had an experience like that once fishing with Joey and Jonathan. We had our worms and were doing well with the number of fish we were catching. They were delighted. I was patting myself on the back for arranging this male bonding time.

Just then, another father and his four children crossed over the small bridge to the spot where we were fishing. His children had come to watch us battle the underwater monsters, which were generally about the size of my hand. I exchanged a nod and hello with my counterpart and continued fishing, but now with an audience.

As the youngsters were entranced, I asked them if they would like to fish too. Their eyes popped open as only kids' eyes can. "Really?" they asked incredulously. "Sure," I said. I was really racking up the points on this one. I stepped away from my own boys to put on a new worm piece for a young girl and explain how to cast with a spinning reel. Just then, I saw something that made me proud.

Joey and Jonathan also began preparing their rods for their new friends. Although the new boys acted like know-it-alls, as most boys and men do, they got squeamish when it came to cutting the worm and sliding the wiggly morsel onto the hook. My boys became like little guides, doing all the jobs the visitors didn't want to do. They gave advice on where to cast, how to react to the nibbles of these tiny fish, and how to safely remove the fish from the hook. They didn't complain. They weren't bossy. They served total strangers and freely shared their time and expertise.

As the apostle Paul wrote to the church at Philippi, "Do nothing out of selfish ambition or vain conceit, but in humility consider others better than yourselves" (Philippians 2:3). If you think about it, the time my kids weren't fishing was a sacrifice on their part. They chose to do it, however, so that they could let others feel the joy we had been experiencing that day. They were thinking about others, not just themselves.

The sun was setting that November day and the temperature was really beginning to drop, so I told the kids it was time to pack up. Our new friends left thanking us all the way to the parking lot. And I was proud. A bit cold, but proud. But when Jonathan asked me to stay a little longer, I remembered how he had thought of others. So, I did the same. We fished and shivered for a few more minutes and they were well worthwhile. I saw it as a reminder for Jonathan that when you do it God's way, you're in for a blessing.

I bet your kids have done something like this too. If you don't think so, maybe you just missed it. Catch them doing something good. Then reward them for it. Let them see the connection between holiness and blessing. Paul gives the Philippians instructions on proper behavior, but also reminds them of the result, "that you may become blameless and pure, children of God without fault in a crooked and depraved generation, in which you shine like stars in the universe" (Philippians 2:15). When your kids are shining, let them see you glow with pride.

Captain's Log: Tonight turn off the TV for a while. This game requires the whole family and their attention. Put a chair in the middle of the room, maybe right in front of the TV, since that's usually the focal point of the living room. That will be the "hot seat." One by one, your family members sit in the hot seat with one direction: they cannot say a word, just listen. Everyone else takes a turn in complimenting the person in the hot seat. Only positive statements are allowed. For instance, I could say, "Shannon, I love the way you make up worship songs. You're really using the gift God gave you to praise him." Or "Jordan, it's amazing to me how you can remember all those Thomas the Tank Engine trains. And the tracks you create in your room are very complicated. It shows you're working hard on them." I won't say, however, that he tends to leave his trains all over his floor, or that they wander into all the other rooms of the house. I'm thinking of others higher than myself, finding the good in others. For some this is tough. For others, listening and having to take a compliment is harder still.

If you think your kids are too old for this, you may want to think again. I used this activity with my high school students and it brought many of these hardened teenagers to tears because it had been so long since they had experienced such an overwhelming sense of love and acceptance.

Use the space provided for your opinion of how the game went with your family. Was it successful? Would you do it again? Why or why not?

A 21-Day Devotional Journal

Captain's Log:

Day Ten

Fishing is for the Faithful

Sundays are reserved for the Lord in our family. We don't fish, but we can talk about fishing and plan our next adventure. By the way, if you like fishing, it's good to have a pastor who enjoys it too. Our pastor was brought up right on the Chesapeake Bay, so the biblical passages that deal with life on the water are not lost. Don't get me wrong—I like a good "seed time and harvest" message, but I get tingly when I hear about "fishers of men."

This Sunday's topic was having the faith to tithe. We've all heard that verse from Malachi (3:10) in which God throws down the proverbial gauntlet, "Test me in this," says the Lord Almighty, "and see if I will not throw open the floodgates of heaven and pour out so much blessing that you will not have room enough for it." I had learned some time ago that there was a difference between giving, tossing in a dollar or five as the offering plate comes around, and tithing. Tithing was intentional, joyful and worshipful. It was a way to show God you mean what you say when you claim to follow him.

But tithing takes faith. Just like fishing. I have never heard my children talk about their aspirations *not* to catch a fish. We don't pack up the van and buy our worms (and candy) for the sole purpose of failure. Rather our ride to the pond is filled with hope, expectation and faith that this time we will catch the biggest fish ever.

Back to the pastor's message. He told the story of a missionary who struggled with the idea of teaching tithing to his new flock. After all, these native people had practically no money, and lived on a barter system. The missionary decided to be true to God's word and teach the important principle. Soon people were tithing their crops, their handmade crafts, whatever they had.

One man arrived early at the church one day carrying a simple fishing pole and a large fish. "I'm paying my tithe," the smiling angler told the missionary. "That's amazing," exclaimed the missionary, "You caught ten fish this size?"

"No, just this one," answered the man, still beaming.

The missionary began to wonder if he man didn't understand the concept of paying a tenth of one's increase and was about to explain it again when the joyous man continued. "But the other nine are out there and I know God is going to give them to me."

That's faith.

We've had some horrible financial times, believe me. But as I look back on them, when I chose to rob God the problems got worse, not better. There were times it looked for sure that our bank account would be overdrawn, or bills wouldn't get paid unless I skipped my tithe, a choice many of us face. We may not see it as dangerous as Daniel and the lion's den or the three Hebrew children in the fiery furnace, and that's the worst part. If satan can attack our faith that God is in control, we become easy prey for all kinds of strife and disappointment.

You believe the fish are out there. You believe you can catch them. So believe the God who made the rivers, lakes and fish when it comes to tithing. "Test me in this" is like God's way of saying, "I double-dog dare you." That's an offer you can't refuse.

Captain's Log: If you're not tithing, start. I know this may be the hardest action item yet, but it's an important one. Not many of us would have the guts to ask our boss for a raise while he knows we've got a hand in the cash register. But that's exactly what we do when we steal God's tithe and ask for a financial breakthough.

By the way, you will never see a good time to start tithing by looking at your checkbook or the pile of bills to pay. If you wait until you think you can do it, you never will.

Chart out a quick budget. List your tithe at the top—assume it's gone—and see what you have left. It may be easier than you think to obey the Lord if you start with the right priorities.

Captain's Log:

Faith, Family and Fishing

Day Eleven

The Fish are Still There Too

A day after the devastating hurricane season of 2005 officially ended, the twenty-sixth named storm was building strength. Residents of Mexico, the United States and all of the islands in between must have been wondering "when will it end?" I can't imagine anyone living in the U.S. who wasn't impacted by the ravaging storms of that year, especially Hurricanes Rita and Katrina.

Aside from soaring gas prices brought on by the destruction of oil refineries and off-shore rigs in the Gulf of Mexico, many churches held clothing drives and provided shelter for the area's evacuees. Colleges offered tuition-free semesters as school-aged children entered new classrooms, some thousands of miles from home. The Red Cross received millions in donations from major corporations, movie stars and everyday heroes. The politicians prepared their publicity tours while arguing who was to blame for the inadequate response that may have cost lives.

Stories about daring rescues and sudden homelessness filled the media airwaves. One particularly poignant story was about a fisherman and his family. Of course, his fishing boat was destroyed along with his home, but those things could be replaced through insurance. The most intriguing part of this story for me was that he was not just unemployed, but unemployable.

This man commented on the dead fish floating in the water, polluted with sewage from the city of New Orleans. Additionally, the broken refinery tanks produced oil-stained waters that would not allow him to fish there for some time. Then I heard the same question I heard after every other major tragedy: Where's God in all of this?

Well, he's right where he's always been. Jesus had promised in Matthew 28:20, "surely I am with you always, to the very end of the age." We don't always see the fish under the water, but we know they're there. In fact, the whole underwater ecosystem rises and falls mostly without our knowledge. Scientists estimate there are over 10,000 species of fish that live at incredible depths that we haven't visited in our most sophisticated submarines. But they're there.

Just like electricity and the wind, we can't see God, but we can see the effects of God in this world. Look at the responses of people in tragic situations. That's where you're likely to see God. God was there when families opened up their doors to kin and stranger alike. God was there as volunteers drove hundreds of miles to serve in the hardest hit areas.

You may have gone through some dark days when it seems like your world has all but unraveled. A divorce, bankruptcy, or death of a child will rock your very foundation. But God is still God; and he's still there.

Just as you check for signs of fish activity in your lakes, you can check for signs of God's activity in your life. When you're listening for him, and watching for him, it seems as though all of creation is supporting you. Friends call you on the phone. Good friends bring over a meal. And your best friend, the one who sticks closer than a brother, promises that the best is yet to come.

Captain's Log: Get a piece of poster board or a large sheet of paper and write across the top: "I know God is near because...." Hang this poster on the refrigerator or on a wall that your family will pass by frequently. You can start off with "He provided the money for the food in the refrigerator." Let each member of the family write something on the poster at their leisure. As more items are listed, they will be read by the passers-by, who will likely write more themselves.

Your poster will soon speak louder than words from the greatest evangelist because it becomes your family's testimony.

Faith, Family and Fishing

Use the space provided to start your own list before adding it to the poster. As you are about half-way through the twenty-one days, look back through your previous entries in the Captain's Log. How have you seen the Lord move in your family? In your church? In your workplace?

Captain's Log:

Day Twelve

Tangled Lines

Before my kids even put a line in the water, I did what any self-respecting father/fisherman would do. I had my kids practice casting in the back yard. The more time they spent practicing, I figured, the less frustration we would have when we actually hit the water. I thought it would take a couple of outings in the hot summer sun to get the feel just right to send their fish-shaped practice lures more than a few feet.

To my surprise, within half an hour, Shannon, Joey and Jonathan were casting their plastic fish over twenty feet with great consistency and some accuracy. To be honest, that's better than I was doing, but I told you about that before.

Feeling accomplished, since I had discovered something that would keep my children happy, occupied and away from the television, I went inside to cool off. Not three casts later, it started: "Dad! My fish got stuck in a tree!"

My first reaction was anger because Jonathan must have been careless. I had told them not to cast too close to the trees. Then, as if on cue, each child's line wove around tree branches across the yard one right after the other. My anger continued until I learned that the reason why they continued to tangle their lines was because they were casting too well. Our yard wasn't big enough for them anymore.

I calmed myself down and even began to chuckle a little, thinking about this excited group of fisher-kids and what a time we'd have at the pond. The next day and the next week, however, the tangles continued. This wasn't good. I told my children that they had proven themselves to be good at casting, too good to be continually ending up in trees. I wanted them to understand their responsibility in the situation. A simple "I'm sorry" and a pledge to be more careful was my desired outcome.

God wants the same thing. "If we confess our sins, he is faithful and just and will forgive us our sins and purify us from all unrighteousness" (1 John 1:9). God's plan is not for us to live under condemnation, or to tremble because God's peering over his glasses down at you with a scowl. (I don't mean to imply God wears glasses, but that's the fear-inducing look I used to get from my second grade teacher.) God's desire is for us to repent—to confess our wrongdoing and turn away from it.

David wrote Psalm 51, after he had committed adultery and conspired in the murder of his mistress' husband. It is really a model of how to seek forgiveness. First, he admits what he has done, "For I know my transgressions, and my sin is always before me. Against you, you only, have I sinned and done what is evil in your sight." (Psalm 51:3-4) All too often today, we shift the blame onto someone (anyone!) who might share the guilt. "It's not my fault," we commonly hear, "it's really...." This is followed by a litany of other usual suspects such as one's parents, socio-economic background, or fast food establishment. Not David—he accepts his responsibility.

He also knows that God *can* forgive him. "Cleanse me with hyssop and I will be clean; wash me and I will be whiter than snow" (Psalm 51:7). Don't let the devil convince you that what you've done is so horrible that God won't forgive you. There's nothing you can do that will erase God's love for you. In my life, I'm usually the last one to forgive myself, so I've struggled in accepting that God has cleansed me. Nevertheless, it doesn't change the fact that he has.

David doesn't stop there, however, because his sights are set on a complete restoration. He prays, "Create in me a pure heart, O God, and renew a steadfast spirit within me" (Psalm 51:10). He longs to bask in the presence of God with the same fervor that he had before, not for his glory but for God's. "Then I will teach transgressors your ways, and sinners will turn back to you" (Psalm 51:13). Think what the world would be like if our children would apologize to you like this: I know I did wrong. I take responsibility. I want to make it right.

Come to think of it, how have your apologies gone recently? This is usually a major issue for men. Once at a church retreat, I saw the power of God move through the hearts of men when they opened up to the idea of forgiveness. It brought out issues I had kept pressed down for 20 years and I called my mother to forgive her for the difficult times we suffered through during my parents' divorce. She began to cry when she told me she had wanted to talk about this for years, but was afraid of what I would say.

Captain's Log: Gentlemen, get into Psalm 51. Read the whole thing. Let it sink into your soul. Let David's passion for renewal become your own. You will see a dramatic change in your life as you seek to forgive and be forgiven. Record a time you were changed by forgiving or being forgiven.

Whether it's someone cutting you off in traffic, your son turning your spinning reel into a 4-lb test bird's nest, or that fight at your mother-in-law's house three years ago, practice forgiveness. And when you have fallen short, don't deny it, accept it and seek forgiveness. It's certainly the most powerful marriage tonic out there, and teaches our children to model themselves after David and not some fast-talking defense attorney.

Captain's Log:

Day Thirteen

The Fish's Point of View

Imagine for a moment how our favorite pastime appears from the perspective of the fish. Early one morning, you are swimming around with some friends from your school (sorry, had to say it). Suddenly, you see a tiny, shimmering shad darting irregularly in front of you. Breakfast. You're guessing by the swim pattern that it is probably injured, so you move in and strike. Excited, you quickly swim back to tell your friends about your kill, forgetting what your mother said about talking with your mouth full.

Then, you feel a sharp pricking in the corner of your mouth. Your movement is stopped. You figure it was that thing you ate, but you're stuck. You can't get it out of your mouth and you can't swim away from it. As much as you fight, you're slipping slowly toward that shadowy blur on top of the water. You've heard about things like this. They told you it would lead to death, but you never thought it would happen to you. The other fish, your schoolmates, have left and are hiding in the deep cover.

In an instant, you are pulled out of the water and are struggling for breath. Still hooked, you would do anything to get free, but it is too late. After spending some time in a dark cooler, your last thought is "Wow, this frying pan is hot."

No, I'm not trying to convince you that fishing is evil, but I am trying to make a connection between the battle we have with fish and the spiritual battle described in Ephesians 6:12. The verse instructs us to put on the whole armor of God to protect ourselves "For our struggle is not against flesh and blood, but against the rulers, against the authorities, against the powers of this dark world and against the spiritual forces of evil in the heavenly realms."

My friend Brian brought this to my attention after a church service one day. He said that there are so many people who fight and complain and argue, but don't even realize the spiritual battle that is going on around them, or that the end has a certain outcome. Unfortunately, many will still be denying God's authority at the Judgment Seat. By that time, it will be too late and they will suffer a fire far worse than a frying pan.

A fish's battle isn't with the lure. It's with the fisherman, who controls the lure and who cast it into the water with one purpose in mind. Fish don't know that. Likewise, many people don't know that satan is holding the lines rigged with sin and temptation. Your fight really may not be with your kids or your wife, it may be a spiritual lure cast by the father of lies for one clear purpose—to destroy your faith and your family.

Before I go on, I should say that I'm not one of those who will attribute any wrong in my life to a direct satanic intervention. "The devil made me do it" is not an excuse I use. Sometimes we make stupid choices and have to suffer the consequences. James 1:14 reminds us that God doesn't tempt us, "but each one is tempted when, by his own evil desire, he is dragged away and enticed." Just as we forgive our children, God forgives us, but there is usually some price to be paid for the wrongdoing. Getting a picture, however, of how the battle lines are drawn helps put in perspective the conflicts we go through each day.

Let me give you some quick examples. Maybe there's somebody at work you can't stand. I had a boss one time whose unofficial job was to make everybody around him just as miserable as he was. He usually succeeded. Everyday I would go in and bear through his tirades with co-workers or on the phone, quick temper and cold demeanor. I never knew that he hated his job and the pressure he was under until I saw him some years later. He was working on his own and had a completely different countenance. He was happy. It dawned on me that my struggle wasn't with my boss, but with my boss's struggle.

On the other side of the coin, maybe there is someone at work you like too much. This woman lights up a room when she comes in. She is stylish, witty and respects the work you do. Your heart skips a beat as you script every word you want to say to her so it sounds perfect. Adultery comes out of feelings like this. Wake up—the woman is the lure, not the cure.

I'm sure my wife will read this one day, and yes, there have been women like that in my workplace too. The book of Proverbs provides solid advice about the entanglements of adultery. The best way off the hook, however, is not to take the bait in the first place. If you're still distracted by the flutter of your heart (enough so that you don't feel the pricking in the side of your mouth), try this: pray for her. It becomes awfully hard to fantasize about a woman you have taken before the throne of grace in prayer.

Wealth, careers, or adulterous thoughts, these lures can be anything that snare us away from the blessed life God has for us. Usually they are not dressed in rags, smelling horribly, but appear to be beautiful and exciting. Recognizing their purpose and the predictable result will help us to avoid them the next time we see that glittering, delicious little morsel darting through the water.

Captain's Log: Has satan set lures out for you? Are you hooked right now? God's word says that he will provide a way out. Your job is to look for it. Prayer (real, honest prayer) is the best remedy for getting unhooked from the snares of sin, when followed up by a holy course of action. You may still have consequences to handle, but you and your mentor can handle that. On one side of the page, write down the ways in which you feel you're snared. On the other, list ways you can avoid temptation, or ways to handle it when the situation arises. Again, work these out with your mentor.

After you have set yourself free, rejoice, but be aware. Understand that satan will likely try another lure similar to the one that just worked. Also, look for ways you can share your success with other men who became entangled, or (better yet) share your testimony so that they won't take the bait.

One more thought on this: don't underestimate the power of your testimony. A friend confided to me that his marriage was in trouble because of his addiction to pornography and phone sex operators. It had gotten so costly that they had missed mortgage payments to cover the phone bills. He was snared when he was just a teenager. It was no big deal. All the kids looked at those magazines. But each time it became a little worse. Eventually, it became a full-blown addiction.

He was relieved when I told him of my similar struggles. I was in no place to judge, but in a perfect place to counsel. God had allowed me to go through temptations and trials so that I could now understand and encourage a friend and help the marriage get back on track.

Captain's Log:

Day Fourteen

Ichthyology and Other Big Words

Okay, I know that ichthyology is the study of fish, but an avid angler knows that being able to identify a fish is only the beginning. The real test is to be able to think like a fish.

You take into consideration the temperature of the water, the cover, and the sky conditions. You may try several color combinations on artificial baits, while also taking into account the presentation. A Texas rig or a Carolina rig?

The really advanced fish psychologists also consult their solunar charts. These charts show the impact of the moon and sun on fish, displaying the best times to catch fish during specific time periods. Although the validity of these charts is highly debated, fish do tend to be drawn to "breakfast" and "dinner" feedings. After all, scientists say that humans do the same thing, and we're animals too. Then the creationist in me charges forth: But God made humans to be superior to animals! True, but we are quick to forget.

In Romans 8:11, Paul reminds us "if the Spirit of him who raised Jesus from the dead is living in you, he who raised Christ from the dead will also give life to your mortal bodies through his Spirit, who lives in you." God didn't make this deal with the fish, or with baby seals, although we seem more committed to protecting their lives than saving our own souls. God made that pledge to us, along with a responsibility. "Therefore, brothers, we have an obligation—but it is not to the sinful nature, to live according to it. For if you live according to the sinful nature, you will die; but if by the Spirit you put to death the misdeeds of the body, you will live." (Romans 8:12-13)

God thinks we're greater than the animals, made for a higher purpose. How about you? Look at the shows we watch on TV. Listen to the songs on the radio. We have turned our lusts for food, material goods and sex into primetime media. Advertisers make millions of dollars during these peak perversion hours because we have shown time and time again it's what we want. I don't believe for a minute that our founding fathers would support pornography under the First Amendment to the Constitution, but again, we pour billions of dollars into the porn industry each year because of our animalistic lusts.

Yes, I know what it's like to be hooked on porn. It's a rush. It's a thrill. Then it's having a hard time looking my wife in the eye, knowing I have been unfaithful to her. Later it's yelling at my kids because the fires of condemnation have consumed my peace. God didn't make me for that. He didn't send his beloved son to die for that. I was like the fish playing dangerously close to the hook because the bait was so tempting. Satan was just waiting for me to strike his line so I could be pulled out of the living water and landed on the shore, flopping around, desperate for life.

At my church, we sing a song that says, "Where the Spirit of the Lord is there is freedom." There's truth in that. Maybe some fish are bound to those solunar charts, but Jesus set us free. We don't have to eat; we can fast. We don't have to fantasize about some computer-aided centerfold; we can experience real intimacy with our wives. We are free indeed.

Captain's Log: A writing assignment today. Make a list of 3 major things that are holding you down: maybe addictions, financial burdens, or illnesses. Take this paper in your hand and pray that the Lord will break these bonds in Jesus' name. Claim your freedom that Jesus bought for you and that satan doesn't want you to collect by destroying the paper.

Be creative and even a bit violent. As Jesus says in Matthew 11:12, "the kingdom of heaven has been forcefully advancing, and forceful men lay hold of it." Get tough with the devil. Rip the paper. Burn it. Nail it to a cross as a reminder of the bloody price that was paid for your freedom.

Each time the temptation comes again to pull you back into old habits, you'll have a vivid reminder of your declaration of liberty. Get some other men together to share this experience and you've got a powerful group of accountability partners. Stand on that word. You are free indeed.

Captain's Log:

Day Fifteen

Name That Fish

If we were to play "Name That Fish," I would lose. I can tell a bluegill from a bass, but that's about it. I take my species charts along in my tackle box so that when we catch something, my kids and I can try to identify it quickly before releasing the catch back into the water. It still amazes me that experienced anglers can tell what type of fish they have even before they bring it out of the water. Those guys can even tell, by looking at its actions under the water, how heavy it is. Usually they estimate correctly within a few ounces.

If you're this type of experienced fisherman, I've got to hand it to you. That's impressive. It requires an incredible amount of detailed knowledge, just like God has about us.

God knows every hair on your head. (Or every hair that used to be on your head.) That can be comforting, but it also can be terrifying. It's comforting to know that the creator of all things, the owner of the cattle on a thousand hills, the one who doesn't even let a swallow fall from the sky without his knowledge, loves me. It's terrifying, however, that this same powerful God knows my faults, failures and sin.

We all have sin. There's just no denying that. And that's the reason why God sent Jesus to carry that burden for us. One of the most dramatic moments in history is when the Son of God hung on the cross, and cried out "My God, My God, why have you forsaken me" (Mark

15:34)? God allowed Jesus to die a painful death, even to turn His holy face away from the darkness of sin—for us. So, what is our response?

This is where God starts to classify us. He is not looking for slight variations like a black crappie or a white crappie, but rather sheep and goats. Look at Matthew 25:31-33:

> When the Son of Man comes in his glory, and all the angels with him, he will sit on his throne in heavenly glory. All the nations will be gathered before him, and he will separate the people one from another as a shepherd separates the sheep from the goats. He will put the sheep on his right and the goats on his left.

This is one of those Biblical scenes I really want to see. That is, of course, providing I'm on the right side. The Sheep (those who followed after Jesus) are rewarded, but the Goats are "cursed [and sent] into the eternal fire prepared for the devil and his angels" (Matthew 25:41). Make no mistake about it. By the time Jesus splits the people into two sides, you are what you are. You can't ask to be traded for a minor leaguer and a player to be named later.

In Matthew 25:35-36, the Bible acts as our trail guide, giving us specific traits of the sheep. The list includes giving food and drink and clothing to people in need, showing hospitality to strangers, caring for the sick and visiting those in prison. From James's epistle, we can add two more, "to look after widows and orphans in their distress and to keep oneself from being polluted by the world" (James 1:27). Salvation comes by grace. We don't earn it, but we can receive it. Once we do, our lives should reflect this gift.

I've been embarrassed by misidentifying fish because there's no quicker way to lose status in the eyes of fellow anglers, but I've never been embarrassed about being a Christian. Paul tells the early church in Rome what we should all remember, "I am not ashamed of the gospel, because it is the power of God for the salvation of everyone who believes: first for the Jew, then for the Gentile." (Romans 1:16)

Sure, I've fallen short and certainly have not been persecuted like Paul. There were times I wondered if my "goat" characteristics outnumbered my "sheep" qualities. But I made a decision to be on that right-hand side. Now, I'm encouraged when people say to me, "I knew you were a Christian when I first met you."

Are you sure of where you stand right now? Are you a Christian only in name, or only on Sundays? I don't know if a smallmouth can become a largemouth through lots of dental work, but I do know that goats can become sheep.

Captain's Log: If you haven't given your heart to the Lord, do so. If you feel that you've been closer to God in the past than you are right now, know that it's not God who's been moving away. Pray for that fire you once had so that you can know beyond any doubt that you're on the right side.

Write down your answers to the following questions: In Matthew 25:35-36, God tells us some of the qualities of the "sheep." Is your faith moving you to sheep-like action?

More to the point, what example of Christian service are you setting for your children to follow?

Captain's Log:

Day Sixteen

The World's Largest Fish Fry

The Bible is full of fish stories. I don't mean things that are untrue; I mean real stories about fish. Until now, we have looked at fishing and seen how it relates to the Bible. In the next few lessons, we'll flip it around and see how the Biblical accounts of fishing still relate to our lives today.

One of the most famous stories from the Bible that involves fish is found in Mark 6:30-44, in which Jesus feeds the 5000 people. Most scholars are estimating that number to be woefully inaccurate, since Bible translations refer to 5000 men, not counting the women and children who also followed Jesus. But you get the idea—it was a lot of people. Just as memorable as the magnitude of the crowd was the menu: five loaves of bread and two fish.

If you've ever tried to fillet a fish, you know that it's not as easy as it looks, until you develop a knack for it. After one trip to the pond, believing that fishing could not only be recreational, but help provide sustenance for my large family, I hacked into my first fish. It was a bass my daughter, Shannon, had caught. Not as big as my 14" bass (okay, 13 ½"), but a respectable fish. I knew we were in trouble on the way home when she not only kissed the fish, in a Jimmy Houston-like way, but she also named the fish. We were going to eat Angela that night.

Admittedly, I did a poor job in separating the meat from the unusable portions of the fish, but I was shocked by how little there was left for me to fry. We all nibbled Angela apprehensively and were glad we had other dishes for dinner. I thought about this passage of scripture and realized why the boy had packed two fish for his lunch. Even for his small appetite, one fish wasn't going to cut it. Yet, when Jesus gave thanks, and passed the food around, they all had more than enough.

I love this story, not just because of the fish, but that it reveals a little-understood part of God's mode of operation. As a child, I heard "Little is much when God's in touch." Think about it. Throughout the Bible, unlikely heroes are called into service against incredible odds with miraculous results. You've got the ineffective general Gideon, the prince-turned-murderer-turned-shepherd Moses, and little orphan Esther. Don't forget Persecutor Paul, Locust-Eater John, or Sinks-like-a-rock Peter. The list goes on and on.

In fact, I would dare you to find an example of a perfectly carved person who lived completely according to God's will, except of course, Jesus. If you did, you wouldn't be able to give God the glory and the praise. This model of perfection would require it. That's why, when you look at yourself, you see your flaws and wonder how God could work with someone like you.

I know my faults. My wife does too. My kids are taking on some of them for their own. (Oh, joy!) Who am I to teach my kids about the Bible? I'm no Bible scholar. *Little is much when God's in touch.* Who am I to think I could have a thriving marriage? My parents got divorced. *Little is much when God's in touch.* Who am I to write this book? I can't solve my problems, let alone anyone else's. *Little is much when God's in touch.*

If God can make a banquet from a couple of panfish, turn water into wine, make blind eyes see, he can make miracles happen in us. The farther away you think you are from a solution, the closer you are to a miracle. That way God's glory is revealed. After all, that's God's M.O.

Captain's Log: You get to be the teacher today. Talk to your kids about the underestimated power in the unlikely things. Consider how the acorn becomes an enormous oak tree, or how rag-tag teams come together to win championships, like the USA's 1980 Olympic ice hockey team. Spend some time showing them how important they are to the operation of your family and your church's ministry. I encourage my boys to perform "chair ministry" (folding up chairs after their Sunday school class). Letting them know they matter now will go a long way in helping them fit in to other environments later. Record the highlights of your discussion here.

Captain's Log:

Day Seventeen

The Jonah in All of Us

You remember Jonah, don't you? It's a whale of a story. (Puns are so hard to resist.) This is one of those stories from the Bible that we learn around age 4 and then don't bother to read the biblical account since we already know what happened. That's a pity too, because there are some interesting things that happen to Jonah after the great fish episode.

Quick review: Jonah, being the man of God that he was, is not happy about his latest assignment. So instead of preaching repentance to the rough and wicked people of Nineveh, he packs his bags and takes the first boat out of town. He recognizes, however, that God is annoyed with his disobedience and asks to be thrown overboard to save the ship from the terrible storm. After being swallowed by a great fish, Jonah has some time to think. Three days later, the fish spits him out and Jonah sets of for Nineveh, wiser and a lot smellier than before.

God asks us to do things that we can't believe. That's usually how we know it is God talking. Sometimes I felt like I could hear his voice so clearly, and other times I felt like my prayers were being sent over a tin can telephone. Like Jonah learning slowly, I began to notice a trend. The times I acted on God's instructions were the times I continued to hear his voice. When I just knew God was off his rocker, and ignored him because I knew better, God became strangely silent. I had done what Paul writes in Romans 1:25, I had "exchanged the truth of God for a lie." God said "yes" and I chose "no."

Before you think, "Great, I've got it; obey God and you won't smell like fish guts," there's more to this story. The book of Jonah doesn't end with a happily ever after life in Nineveh. In fact, in Chapter 4, Jonah is angry at God for not destroying the city. He knew God's mercy and is fuming because he went through his ordeal while God is just going to spare the lives of the sinful people anyway. He yells at God, "O Lord, is this not what I said when I was still at home" (Jonah 4:2)? Later he shouts, "Now, O Lord, take away my life, for it is better for me to die than to live" (Jonah 4:3).

Jonah pouts outside the city waiting for the destruction he feels is necessary, but it never comes. Instead, our long-suffering God provides a vine that shades Jonah's balding head from the hot sun. The Bible says that Jonah likes that. The next day, however, when God sends a worm to eat the vine, Jonah is back in the ring ready to fight.

God asks him the simple question, "But God said to Jonah, 'Do you have a right to be angry about the vine?'" Jonah responds in his arrogant way, "'I do,' he said. 'I am angry enough to die.'" (Jonah 4:9) Forget that God had saved him from the great fish. Forget that God saved him from the destruction of the city. Jonah wanted it done his way, not God's way.

God calmly reminds Jonah that he was neither responsible for growing the vine, nor was he responsible for the creation of the people of Nineveh, but God was. God, therefore, had every right and responsibility to care for his own.

There is a little Jonah in all of us, from our outright disobedience of God's instructions to our refusal to see things his way. We'd rather get a lawyer to settle the score than seek God's wisdom. Jonah yells at God, and sometimes I do too. But notice that God never corrects Jonah for this. In fact, God continues to speak to Jonah and care for him.

God wants communication with us. He wants to know our real feelings and concerns. When you don't understand God's plan, tell him. Shout at him. It's far better than keeping quiet, letting the problems of the world digest you.

Captain's Log: Have a heart-to-heart with God today. Let him know exactly what's going on in your life. Ask him what you really want to know about your future and how to serve him. I used to tell my students that I can't steer a parked car, meaning that as long as they were trying, I could help them. God works the same way. As long as Jonah was in communication with God, even when he was going in the wrong direction, God could still influence him. Use the page provided to take notes for your conversation and make sure to write down God's answers to your questions. It may not come as an audible response, but check your spirit. You'll know what God's message is for you.

Captain's Log:

Day Eighteen

Perfect Storms, Imperfect People

Every time I mention to Jonathan the possibility of fishing from a boat, he shakes his head and responds with one word: sharks.

It is as though I forced him to watch <u>The Perfect Storm</u> over and over again so that he is deathly afraid of the monsters lurking in the Susquehanna River. Nevertheless, he is determined to stay on the shore. Don't misunderstand me; I'm not judging Jonathan. In fact, I was a bit nervous the first time I went fishing in the ocean. Although we had great weather and didn't stay for long, in the back of my mind I wondered how I would do in a tempest. Probably not well.

The seafarers in Jesus' day were no doubt hearty men. It was a family business, like Zebedee and Sons. These men were aware of the risks and still ventured out to the seas to make their livelihood. So when we read about the disciples being terrified in the midst of a storm, we can assume it was horrifying. "A squall came down on the lake, so that the boat was being swamped, and they were in great danger." (Luke 8:23)

Meanwhile, Jesus, the one who suggested this three hour tour, was asleep on the deck, enjoying the misty breeze. Certain that Jesus didn't know the gravity of the situation, they "woke him, saying, 'Master, Master, we're going to drown'" (Luke 8:24). Come on, Jesus, get a handle on reality here!

The Lord's reaction is perfect (naturally). "He got up and rebuked the wind and the raging waters; the storm subsided, and all was calm. 'Where is your faith?' he asked his disciples." (Luke 8:25)

I could have been on that boat. In fact, I've been in situations much like that in my life. They were the most dreadful experiences of my life, times I knew God had forgotten about me. As I reminded God of my agony, he seemed to say, "Tony, where is your faith?" as he blew the situation away with a gentle breath. We can get so worked up over things that are nothing to God. We stress, rant, throw things and growl like dogs, but God's already got it figured out.

Like the disciples, we've been down. And like the disciples, we've been up. On another night at sea, Jesus tells Peter to walk out on to the rough waves. Peter steps out of the boat and is aghast because this time *he* is the miracle. This fisherman who has spent a lifetime on the water, is now literally *on* the water. Can you imagine the mixture of wonder and power Peter felt at that time?

There have been days I felt like I could save the world if I just had a microphone loud enough. I felt the presence of God so strongly that I pitied anyone coming too close to me. I would be the first to shout "Amen!" These are the days when you feel like walking on water is a real possibility. But like Peter, who takes his eyes off of the Lord and is blinded by his circumstances, I would lose sight of God's presence and sink back into the waves of lukewarm Christianity.

Again, like Peter, Jesus would pick me up and bring me back to the boat. This, by the way, is the most fascinating part of the story for me. It's a point that few pastors bring up: Peter gets back in the boat. Life goes on.

Follow me on this. Be it a high point in your spiritual life, when you are the most righteous overcomer God ever created, or be it the nadir of your walk, when God reaches down to pull you out of the mud, you still get back in the boat. The fuzzy feelings and echoes of your praise song are gone. Now what do you do? Are you living like you've done the miraculous, or is that just a memory for the scrapbook? Do you remember the depths of your sorrow, or are you comforted that you're over that now?

God is good. All the time. He allows us to go through peaks and valleys for a reason. There is more living ahead and you will need the experience you've gained to make the most of the days to come. So climb back into that boat, but don't forget the taste of the salt water.

One step or one stumble, that's how you build your faith.

Captain's Log: Divide today's page into two sides. The left side is for times you felt spiritually invincible. The right side is for those moments you were wallowing in the muck. List 3-5 examples on each side and reflect on them. What have you learned from those episodes? Why do you think the Lord allowed them to happen in your life? Has anyone (including you) actually benefited from a severe trial or struggle? If you could change these past events, would you? Why or why not?

Captain's Log:

Day Nineteen

Breakfast on the Beach

The apostle Peter is my favorite person in the Bible. Here is a guy who knows his shortcomings, who has enjoyed the highs of walking on water, and suffered the lows of knowing he denied Christ. After all that, when he's hanging out with his friends in the twenty-first chapter of John's gospel, he decides to go fishing.

They fish all night and catch nothing. Probably feeling guilty about that morning of the crucifixion, Peter's thinking, "Just my luck. This is God getting back at me." At that moment, he hears someone suggest casting their nets on the other side of the boat. "The last time someone told me to do that," Peter reflects, "it was...Jesus!" They hoist up a net full of fish and realize the Lord has done it again.

Peter wastes no time with the fish, however. "As soon as Simon Peter heard him say, 'It is the Lord,' he wrapped his outer garment around him (for he had taken it off) and jumped into the water" (John 21:7). Peter is a passionate man. This time his passion is exuberance for the Lord. It's like the good old days, when Peter felt loved and secure in his position as a disciple. In the light of Jesus, everything else—even a boat full of fish—seems unimportant.

As they begin to eat their breakfast on the shore, Jesus asks Peter three times, "Do you love me?" To each time, Peter responds "yes," but the Bible says that Peter was getting a little upset by the third time Jesus asked the question. "How many times is he going to ask me this?" Peter likely wondered. The same number of times you denied him, Peter. Jesus fully restores Peter to his solid foundation, a rock on dry land, preparing for that day he will preach to over 3000 people in Acts Chapter Two.

It's as though his entire life up until this moment has been some divine job interview and Peter has proven himself worthy. By worldly accounts, he has proven himself unpredictable, unreliable, and uneducated. But his worth comes from the fact that Jesus loves him and restores him to the powerful man he is meant to be.

Your worth comes from the same source. God isn't impressed by our job titles, our bank accounts, or educational degrees. He isn't hoping that we will all turn out to be Bible trivia experts. He wants us to know him and to know the purpose he has for us as husbands and fathers. I've heard one non-biblical definition of hell is the person you are meeting the person you could have been. None of us are where we want to be spiritually, but there's no time for lamenting lost opportunities. You've got a job to do.

Throughout these readings, you have been challenged to be honest with yourself and honest with God. You've been prompted to set godly goals and steer free from temptation and the bondage of sin. You've prayed and been forgiven. All of these other devotions dealt with you and your relationships with God, your family and your community. But now you're on to the most important task yet: feeding the sheep.

Jesus gave Peter the task three times after Peter affirmed that he loved the Lord. And Jesus charges us with the same. You are the shepherd of your family. When the wolves come to attack, you are not only the one your family turns to, you are the one God has ordained for the job. Real men—read on for more reasons why you are "da man."

Captain's Log: Sheep are notoriously weak animals. They constantly need to be led, fed and protected. This makes the shepherd's job much more difficult. Patience, bravery and resourcefulness are, therefore, necessary virtues to be a good shepherd. Consider the fact that great Biblical leaders David and Moses spent time as shepherds.

Write your responses to these questions: Do you think Peter possessed these qualities? If not, how and when did Peter change? (See

Acts chapters 1 and 2 for more information.)

How about you? Would you receive a good report from your sheep? If you're brave enough, go ask them.

Captain's Log:

Day Twenty

You Da Man—Part One
Your Wife Doesn't Need a Man of the World

All of the readings up to this point have been a lead-up to these last two. I figured that if you've stayed with me so far, I'm not going to lose you now, so I'm going to give you the real deal—the trophy catch you mount on your wall.

I don't know if you got the memo, but the American man is under attack. Don't believe me? Turn on the television and show me a good example of a man on any of the current programs. Find one who is the head of the home, who is obeyed by his children and respected by his wife. I don't mean reruns of "Father Knows Best" or "Leave It to Beaver." You won't be able to do it. That's one reason why I like watching the Sportsman Channel with my kids, especially my boys. Sure, I've seen some goofy characters there, but most are men being men: hunting, fishing, exploring the wilderness. I really love it when they show men sharing these adventures with their kids.

Like many children, mine like cartoons. Like many men, I do too. Nevertheless, I have noticed a clear theme that runs through cartoon (and sitcom) families. The man is stupid. The woman really runs the family. The kids know it and therefore are left to make their own rules, thinking they are smarter than their parents are. What's worse, usually the shows prove the kids to be right.

I don't want to be a man of the world. I want to be like Joshua. Look at his book in the Bible sometime and get a feel for the kind of man he was. Joshua was one of the two guys who spied on the Canaanites and came back ready to attack, not cowering in fear like the other ten. He was more fearful of disobeying God than of some army, even though the Canaanites seemed a powerful foe. "Only do not rebel against the Lord. And do not be afraid of the people of the land, because we will swallow them up." (Numbers 14:9) Then he makes one of his many defining statements, "Their protection is gone, but the Lord is with us. Do not be afraid of them." (Numbers 14:9)

From the beginning of the book of Joshua, when God says, "Moses is dead. Joshua, you da man," (Joshua 1:1, my translation), Joshua takes his orders from the Lord. Attack this nation. Done. Conquer this land. Done. Near the end of his life, he draws the line in the sand with another essential verse, one that reads like a mission statement for Christian men everywhere, "choose for yourselves this day whom you will serve...But as for me and my household, we will serve the Lord." (Joshua 24:15)

Moreover, Paul's letter to the Ephesians is packed with truth you will never hear on Oprah or Dr. Phil, but will teach you how to become a Joshua-like man. This is where that passage about wives submitting to their husbands comes in. Some people have told me that their wives won't submit to them. Mine didn't either, until I became the man she could submit to. Read through Ephesians 5:22-27:

> Wives, submit to your husbands as to the Lord. For the husband is the head of the wife as Christ is head of the church, his body, of which he is the Savior. Now as the church submits to Christ, so also wives should submit to their husbands in everything. Husbands, love your wives, just as Christ loved the church and gave himself up for her to make her holy, cleansing her by the washing with water through the word, and to present her to himself as a radiant church, without stain or wrinkle or any other blemish, but holy and blameless.

Men, you've got the bigger job here. You've got to love her so much you would go to the cross for her. If you're struggling with putting the toilet seat down, you may have a long way to go. You are required to go all out for her, so that she may be blameless before the Lord. Step up and take the lead. Prove to her that you are a man worth following because you are a man with her best interests in mind. Demonstrate by your words and actions that you take your orders from the Lord, not the world. (Guess that would require more prayer time to receive those orders, huh?)

God made man and woman. He made them to come together in marriage, but our society (and satan) are working vigorously to destroy what God has created for good. Writers like Steve Ferrar and John Eldridge are producing great books to counteract this effort, but in your house, it comes down to you. The fate of your family is placed on your shoulders. Nervous? Remember what Joshua said, "Their protection is gone, but the Lord is with us. Do not be afraid of them." You're in the thick of the battle, but the Lord has got your back.

God chose you for this assignment. He made you the man.

Captain's Log: Ask yourself: Are you pleasing God or pleasing man? What is the hierarchy of your home? (Is it God first, Dad, Mom and then kids, or is something out of whack?) Take some time to think about this and write down your response. God gave us directions on how the family should be established. We've just refused to follow them and we've paid the price with incredible divorce rates, rampant homosexuality and confused children.

If you don't already have a mentor, find one. This man may be a church elder, bible group leader, or close friend, preferably one who has a strong relationship with the Lord and with his family. Check the fruit on the tree and if he's got the kind of family you want, you've found your mentor. He may be able to give you a better picture of how your family is really operating and give you advice on how correctly to align it.

Pick one of the gospels and study each time people said Jesus spoke with authority. He was no wimp. The table turning in the temple was just one episode. Fighting the devil face to face takes real power.

Truthfully, my wife was waiting for me to lead. She even asked me on some occasions to step up and make decisions, to take control. I didn't know what that meant or how to do it. In my conversations with other men, they've shared similar experiences. My mentor has been instrumental in helping me to grow a backbone like Joshua—to be the man.

Your wife needs you to be the head, so she can fulfill her responsibility to submit to you. Your kids need it too, as you will see in the next reading.

Captain's Log:

Day Twenty-One

You Da Man—Part Two
A Dad after God's Own Heart

When you keep reading in Ephesians, you get to chapter 6, which begins, "Children obey your parents in the Lord, for this is right." (Ephesians 6:1) That's strange, but that's not what I see being practiced on sitcoms or sung in music lyrics or posted on the internet. We're so busy fighting the power that obedience is a dirty word. I've heard, "Won't this hurt their individuality?" Nope. God said it was right. Ephesians continues, "'Honor your father and mother'—which is the first commandment with a promise—'that it may go well with you and that you may enjoy long life on the earth'" (Ephesians 6:2-3). See, when you said that it was for their own good, you were right.

Based on these verses, and the commandment "Thou shalt not lie," we would spank our children if the offense fell into three categories: disobedience, disrespect or dishonesty. I made up my mind. I was going to do it God's way. When you think about it, these children are yours to care for during a short period of time. And since the Bible tells us "You are not your own; you were bought at a price" (1 Corinthians 6:19-20), then our kids really aren't ours either. So in essence, we should remember we are raising God's kids. What God is looking for, then, is a Dad after his own heart.

I knew a Dad who loved to go fishing and went often. He would spend a great amount of time and money to take the trips that would usually last for an entire weekend. And his boys stayed home. Think about the message that sent. I'm sure he loved his sons, but I am convinced that fishing with my kids is more about bringing up God's kids and less about drowning worms.

God wants you to discipline them (see Proverbs 13:24), but not to be hypocritical or drive them nuts, "Fathers do not exasperate your children; instead, bring them up in the training and instruction of the Lord" (Ephesians 6:4). He tells you to teach them through your words, actions and behaviors.

My boys need to learn how to be men. That's why God made me. They need to see that, contrary to popular media, a man doesn't have to cheat on his wife or his taxes. He doesn't have to be drunk, abusive or lazy. A man can cry. A man can go to church and dance before the Lord. A man can be tender enough to care for a newborn baby, or rough enough for tackle football. Most of all, a man bears the responsibility of his family's security and through obedience to the Lord, obtains it.

My sons also get an on-going lesson on how to treat a woman. I secretly love it when my kids moan when they see my wife and me kissing. It tells me they caught me demonstrating love, so they'll be more apt to do that in their marriage. Sex is great—in marriage—the way God designed it. That's a lesson boys need to hear from Dad.

On the other side, my daughters are getting used to a man's way of thinking, as obscure as it seems to them, so it won't be a shock when they begin their own families. To that end, I've also taken my older daughter out on dates. I open the door for her, let her pick the movie and the seats. Okay, I'm really trying to set the bar so high that she won't waste time with losers. While I haven't yet introduced her younger brothers as "Smith, Wesson, Winchester and Colt," I still have that card to play too.

I compliment my daughters on their appearance, especially when they are dressed conservatively so they develop a pattern connecting modesty with high esteem. I've had many high school students in my classes who came to school provocatively dressed. I would usually make comments privately to them about buttoning a few more buttons on their shirts. Or, I'd tell them while their skirts may be appropriate for some stages in Baltimore, they are not appropriate for our high school auditorium. Many of them started calling me Dad. The sad part was that some of them had Dads at home. The sadder part was that others did not.

The Lord God Almighty has given you the authority to be the man. I firmly believe that good dads are needed to rise up and serve their families, and also to act as role models for other children being raised by single mothers. In one instance, while we had a single mom and her two kids living with us, I returned from a business trip. My kids flew out the front door, shouting "Daddy! Daddy!" Right in the middle of them was my little two-year old godchild, Olivia, shouting "Daddy!" and racing to get her hug too. If she's got no other Daddy, then I'll do it with honor. After all, they're all God's kids anyway.

Captain's Log: If the weight of your family won't get you on your knees to pray, I don't know what will. Pray. Pray for God's wisdom (James 1:5) and his direction (Proverbs 3:5-6). Pray for the blessings of Deuteronomy chapter 28. Pray for future generations of your family. You are the man. You are the patriarch. Write your prayer for the generations of your family that are to come. Then pray it—fervently. Your family is at stake.

A 21-Day Devotional Journal

Captain's Log:

Epilogue

If you are reading this before you have read all the other lessons, shame on you.

If you are reading this after completing the 21-day devotional series, you have accomplished something significant in your spiritual growth. Congratulations! But don't stop now. Grab another book, sign up for some email devotionals, something that will keep you growing in God's word.

I have heard that a shark has to keep moving forward or else it will die. It's the same with Christians. Either we're striving to live for Jesus, or living for our complacency. The Bible uses the word "perish" to describe this kind of death. No, we won't actually fall down dead if we miss reading the Bible, but we begin to rot like a banana. We ripen past our prime and become that dark brown mush that leaves sticky ooze on the countertop. (Well, I mean...not that we would have any experience with rotten bananas at our house.)

I pray this book has been an encouragement to you and has strengthened your commitments to your family and your Lord. If it has, please contact me. I'd love to hear from you.

Until then, leave some of the big ones in the pond for me.

Resources for Reel Men

The following websites represent some of the best fishing ministries that I've found. To be fair, I'm sure it's not a complete list, but I've gotten to know some of these folks and the passion with which they fish and worship the Lord.

Hooked for Life Ministries (www.hookedforlife.org)

This organization, directed by Trevor Ruble (who was kind enough to write the foreword to this book) and Jerry Stoneking, Jr., is unique because of its emphasis on outreach to children and families. Hooked for Life provides a complete curriculum with detailed lesson plans for a fishing club meeting on a regular basis, a VBS setting, and even a one-day project. Trevor and Jerry do a great job following through with the purpose behind our God-given passion to fish.

Fishers of Men National Tournament Trail (www.fomntt.com)

Pro fishing tours can be exciting, but not always the best place for your family. If your involvement in a fishing tournament is limited due to the corporate sponsors of the event, check out Fishers of Men. Not only do they provide some serious competition and spectacular prizes, but their rules of conduct are written to support families. With 50 divisions in 26 states (at the time of printing), Fishers of Men is large enough to command respect, but hasn't lost sight of the real mission their name reflects. Meetings before the tournament provide an excellent opportunity for evangelism.

Christian Anglers' Association (www.christiananglers.net)

Founded by Dr. Tom Rakow, the founder of Christian Deer Hunters Association, the CAA offers an opportunity for fishermen to interact and receive some great inspirational literature. This literature not only includes devotional books, but cards and tracts for sharing the saving power of God through Jesus Christ.

God's Great Outdoors (www.ggoutdoors.org)

From great products to conferences and retreats to wild game recipes submitted from across the country, Gerry Caillouet's ministry is almost a one-stop shop for Christian sportsmen on the internet. You can also listen to his terrific radio program online.

Christian Outdoorsman (www.christianoutdoorsman.com)

Looking for a fishing buddy in your area? Need some tips for that new lake you're fishing next weekend? Christian Outdoorsman may give you the answers you're looking for. This site acts as a meeting place for sportsmen, as well as a source for information and the latest gear.

Contact Tony Gerdes online at

www.reelman.org

or by mail at:

reelman.org
172 Sycamore Trail
Delta, PA 17314